AF808789

Welcome to the Corporate Growth Journal

This 90-day journal is designed to help professionals pause, reflect, and grow—both personally and as a team. In today's fast-paced work environment, clarity and connection are often sacrificed. This journal creates intentional space to reset, slow down, refocus, and thrive with intention.

Created with purpose by CMD Unlimited, LLC

At CMD Unlimited, LLC, we specialize in journaling tools that support productivity, gratitude, and growth —especially during seasons of change. Our goal is to help individuals and teams navigate transitions with clarity, intention, and purpose.

CMDUnlimitedLLC.org | CMDUnlimitedLLC@yahoo.com

Day 1

Date: ______________________

Today's Meeting & Time ____

Follow-Up Calls /Emails ____

Follow-Up Calls /Emails ____

How am I feeling this morning and why?

____

____

____

____

Top 2 Priorities and Focus for today

____

____

____

My Personal Growth and Development Goals for today

____

____

____

Team Collaboration Notes Who did I support or collaborate with today?

____

____

____

Gratitude in the Workplace What went well? Who and what am I thankful for today?

____

____

____

____

____

Goals for tomorrow

____

____

____

"Success is the sum of small efforts, repeated day in and day out."

Day 2

Date: ______________________

Today's Meeting & Time ____

Follow-Up Calls /Emails ____

Follow-Up Calls /Emails ____

How am I feeling this morning and why?

____

____

____

____

Top 2 Priorities and Focus for today

____

____

____

My Personal Growth and Development Goals for today

____

____

____

Team Collaboration Notes Who did I support or collaborate with today?

____

____

____

Gratitude in the Workplace What went well? Who and what am I thankful for today?

____

____

____

____

____

Goals for tomorrow

____

____

____

"The only way to do great work is to love what you do."

Day 3

Date: ______________________

Today's Meeting & Time ____

Follow-Up Calls /Emails ____

Follow-Up Calls /Emails ____

How am I feeling this morning and why?

____

____

____

____

Top 2 Priorities and Focus for today

____

____

____

My Personal Growth and Development Goals for today

____

____

____

Team Collaboration Notes Who did I support or collaborate with today?

____

____

____

Gratitude in the Workplace What went well? Who and what am I thankful for today?

____

____

____

____

____

Goals for tomorrow

____

____

____

"Believe you can and you're halfway there."

Day 4

Date: ______________________

Today's Meeting & Time ____

Follow-Up Calls /Emails ____

Follow-Up Calls /Emails ____

How am I feeling this morning and why?

____

____

____

____

Top 2 Priorities and Focus for today

____

____

____

My Personal Growth and Development Goals for today

____

____

____

Team Collaboration Notes Who did I support or collaborate with today?

____

____

____

Gratitude in the Workplace What went well? Who and what am I thankful for today?

____

____

____

____

____

Goals for tomorrow

____

____

____

"Don't watch the clock; do what it does. Keep going."

Day 5

Date: ____________________

Today's Meeting & Time ____________________

Follow-Up Calls /Emails ____________________

Follow-Up Calls /Emails ____________________

How am I feeling this morning and why?

____

____

____

____

Top 2 Priorities and Focus for today

____

____

____

My Personal Growth and Development Goals for today

____

____

____

Team Collaboration Notes Who did I support or collaborate with today?

____

____

____

Gratitude in the Workplace What went well? Who and what am I thankful for today?

____

____

____

____

____

Goals for tomorrow

____

____

____

"Hard work beats talent when talent doesn't work hard."

Day 6

Date: ____________________

Today's Meeting & Time ____________________

Follow-Up Calls /Emails ____________________

Follow-Up Calls /Emails ____________________

How am I feeling this morning and why?

____

____

____

____

Top 2 Priorities and Focus for today

____

____

____

My Personal Growth and Development Goals for today

____

____

____

Team Collaboration Notes Who did I support or collaborate with today?

____

____

____

Gratitude in the Workplace What went well? Who and what am I thankful for today?

____

____

____

____

____

Goals for tomorrow

____

____

____

"Your work is going to fill a large part of your life."

Day 7

Date: ____________________

Today's Meeting & Time ____

Follow-Up Calls /Emails ____

Follow-Up Calls /Emails ____

How am I feeling this morning and why?

____

____

____

____

Top 2 Priorities and Focus for today

____

____

____

My Personal Growth and Development Goals for today

____

____

____

Team Collaboration Notes Who did I support or collaborate with today?

____

____

____

Gratitude in the Workplace What went well? Who and what am I thankful for today?

____

____

____

____

____

Goals for tomorrow

____

____

____

"Excellence is not a skill. It is an attitude."

Day 8

Date: ______________________

Today's Meeting & Time ____

Follow-Up Calls /Emails ____

Follow-Up Calls /Emails ____

How am I feeling this morning and why?

____

____

____

____

Top 2 Priorities and Focus for today

____

____

____

My Personal Growth and Development Goals for today

____

____

____

Team Collaboration Notes Who did I support or collaborate with today?

____

____

____

Gratitude in the Workplace What went well? Who and what am I thankful for today?

____

____

____

____

____

Goals for tomorrow

____

____

____

"Quality means doing it right when no one is looking."

Day 9

Date: ______________________

Today's Meeting & Time ____

Follow-Up Calls /Emails ____

Follow-Up Calls /Emails ____

How am I feeling this morning and why?

____

____

____

____

Top 2 Priorities and Focus for today

____

____

____

My Personal Growth and Development Goals for today

____

____

____

Team Collaboration Notes Who did I support or collaborate with today?

____

____

____

Gratitude in the Workplace What went well? Who and what am I thankful for today?

____

____

____

____

____

Goals for tomorrow

____

____

____

"The best way to predict the future is to create it."

Day 10

Date: ______________________

Today's Meeting & Time ______________________

Follow-Up Calls /Emails ______________________

Follow-Up Calls /Emails ______________________

How am I feeling this morning and why?

____

____

____

____

Top 2 Priorities and Focus for today

____

____

____

My Personal Growth and Development Goals for today

____

____

____

Team Collaboration Notes Who did I support or collaborate with today?

____

____

____

Gratitude in the Workplace What went well? Who and what am I thankful for today?

____

____

____

____

____

Goals for tomorrow

____

____

____

"Act as if what you do makes a difference. It does."

Day 11

Date: ______________________

Today's Meeting & Time ____

Follow-Up Calls /Emails ____

Follow-Up Calls /Emails ____

How am I feeling this morning and why?

____

____

____

____

Top 2 Priorities and Focus for today

____

____

____

My Personal Growth and Development Goals for today

____

____

____

Team Collaboration Notes Who did I support or collaborate with today?

____

____

____

Gratitude in the Workplace What went well? Who and what am I thankful for today?

____

____

____

____

____

Goals for tomorrow

____

____

____

"Strive not to be a success, but rather to be aof value."

Day 12

Date: ________________________

Today's Meeting & Time ____

Follow-Up Calls /Emails ____

Follow-Up Calls /Emails ____

How am I feeling this morning and why?

Top 2 Priorities and Focus for today

My Personal Growth and Development Goals for today

Team Collaboration Notes Who did I support or collaborate with today?

Gratitude in the Workplace What went well? Who and what am I thankful for today?

Goals for tomorrow

"Success usually comes to those who are too busy to be looking for it."

Day 13

Date: ____________________

Today's Meeting & Time ____________________

Follow-Up Calls /Emails ____________________

Follow-Up Calls /Emails ____________________

How am I feeling this morning and why?

Top 2 Priorities and Focus for today

My Personal Growth and Development Goals for today

Team Collaboration Notes Who did I support or collaborate with today?

Gratitude in the Workplace What went well? Who and what am I thankful for today?

Goals for tomorrow

"The harder you work for something, the greater you'll feel when you achieve it."

Day 14

Date: ______________________

Today's Meeting & Time ____

Follow-Up Calls /Emails ____

Follow-Up Calls /Emails ____

How am I feeling this morning and why?

____
____
____
____

Top 2 Priorities and Focus for today

____
____
____

My Personal Growth and Development Goals for today

____
____
____

Team Collaboration Notes Who did I support or collaborate with today?

____
____
____

Gratitude in the Workplace What went well? Who and what am I thankful for today?

____
____
____
____
____

Goals for tomorrow

____
____
____

"Success isn't just about what you accomplish, but what you inspire others to do."

Day 15

Date: ______________________

Today's Meeting & Time ____

Follow-Up Calls /Emails ____

Follow-Up Calls /Emails ____

How am I feeling this morning and why?

____

____

____

____

Top 2 Priorities and Focus for today

____

____

____

My Personal Growth and Development Goals for today

____

____

____

Team Collaboration Notes Who did I support or collaborate with today?

____

____

____

Gratitude in the Workplace What went well? Who and what am I thankful for today?

____

____

____

____

____

Goals for tomorrow

____

____

____

"Opportunities don't happen. You create them."

Day 16

Date: ____________________

Today's Meeting & Time ____

Follow-Up Calls /Emails ____

Follow-Up Calls /Emails ____

How am I feeling this morning and why?

____

____

____

____

Top 2 Priorities and Focus for today

____

____

____

My Personal Growth and Development Goals for today

____

____

____

Team Collaboration Notes Who did I support or collaborate with today?

____

____

____

Gratitude in the Workplace What went well? Who and what am I thankful for today?

____

____

____

____

____

Goals for tomorrow

____

____

____

"Don't limit your challenges. Challenge your limits."

Day 17

Date: ______________________

Today's Meeting & Time ____

Follow-Up Calls /Emails ____

Follow-Up Calls /Emails ____

How am I feeling this morning and why?

____

____

____

____

Top 2 Priorities and Focus for today

____

____

____

My Personal Growth and Development Goals for today

____

____

____

Team Collaboration Notes Who did I support or collaborate with today?

____

____

____

Gratitude in the Workplace What went well? Who and what am I thankful for today?

____

____

____

____

____

Goals for tomorrow

____

____

____

"Dream big."

Day 18

Date: ____________________

Today's Meeting & Time ____________________

Follow-Up Calls /Emails ____________________

Follow-Up Calls /Emails ____________________

How am I feeling this morning and why?

Top 2 Priorities and Focus for today

My Personal Growth and Development Goals for today

Team Collaboration Notes Who did I support or collaborate with today?

Gratitude in the Workplace What went well? Who and what am I thankful for today?

Goals for tomorrow

"Each day is a canvas for your masterpiece."

Day 19

Date: ______________________

Today's Meeting & Time ____

Follow-Up Calls /Emails ____

Follow-Up Calls /Emails ____

How am I feeling this morning and why?

____

____

____

____

Top 2 Priorities and Focus for today

____

____

____

My Personal Growth and Development Goals for today

____

____

____

Team Collaboration Notes Who did I support or collaborate with today?

____

____

____

Gratitude in the Workplace What went well? Who and what am I thankful for today?

____

____

____

____

____

Goals for tomorrow

____

____

____

"Great things never come from comfort zones."

Day 20

Date: ____________________

Today's Meeting & Time ____

Follow-Up Calls /Emails ____

Follow-Up Calls /Emails ____

How am I feeling this morning and why?

____

____

____

____

Top 2 Priorities and Focus for today

____

____

____

My Personal Growth and Development Goals for today

____

____

____

Team Collaboration Notes Who did I support or collaborate with today?

____

____

____

Gratitude in the Workplace What went well? Who and what am I thankful for today?

____

____

____

____

____

Goals for tomorrow

____

____

____

"Push yourself, because no one else is going to do it for you."

Day 21

Date: ______________________

Today's Meeting & Time ____

Follow-Up Calls /Emails ____

Follow-Up Calls /Emails ____

How am I feeling this morning and why?

____

____

____

____

Top 2 Priorities and Focus for today

____

____

____

My Personal Growth and Development Goals for today

____

____

____

Team Collaboration Notes Who did I support or collaborate with today?

____

____

____

Gratitude in the Workplace What went well? Who and what am I thankful for today?

____

____

____

____

____

Goals for tomorrow

____

____

____

"Your limitation - it's up to you."

Day 22

Date: ______________________

Today's Meeting & Time ____

Follow-Up Calls /Emails ____

Follow-Up Calls /Emails ____

How am I feeling this morning and why?

____

____

____

____

Top 2 Priorities and Focus for today

____

____

____

My Personal Growth and Development Goals for today

____

____

____

Team Collaboration Notes Who did I support or collaborate with today?

____

____

____

Gratitude in the Workplace What went well? Who and what am I thankful for today?

____

____

____

____

____

Goals for tomorrow

____

____

____

"Sometimes later becomes never. Act now."

Day 23

Date: ____________________

Today's Meeting & Time ____________________

Follow-Up Calls /Emails ____________________

Follow-Up Calls /Emails ____________________

How am I feeling this morning and why?

____

____

____

____

Top 2 Priorities and Focus for today

____

____

____

My Personal Growth and Development Goals for today

____

____

____

Team Collaboration Notes Who did I support or collaborate with today?

____

____

____

Gratitude in the Workplace What went well? Who and what am I thankful for today?

____

____

____

____

____

Goals for tomorrow

____

____

____

"Work in silence, and let your success be your noise."

Day 24

Date: ______________________

Today's Meeting & Time ____

Follow-Up Calls /Emails ____

Follow-Up Calls /Emails ____

How am I feeling this morning and why?

____

____

____

____

Top 2 Priorities and Focus for today

____

____

____

My Personal Growth and Development Goals for today

____

____

____

Team Collaboration Notes Who did I support or collaborate with today?

____

____

____

Gratitude in the Workplace What went well? Who and what am I thankful for today?

____

____

____

____

____

Goals for tomorrow

____

____

____

"Don't be busy, be productive."

Day 25

Date: ______________________

Today's Meeting & Time ____

Follow-Up Calls /Emails ____

Follow-Up Calls /Emails ____

How am I feeling this morning and why?

Top 2 Priorities and Focus for today

My Personal Growth and Development Goals for today

Team Collaboration Notes Who did I support or collaborate with today?

Gratitude in the Workplace What went well? Who and what am I thankful for today?

Goals for tomorrow

"Big moves begin with small steps."

Day 26

Date: ______________________

Today's Meeting & Time ____

Follow-Up Calls /Emails ____

Follow-Up Calls /Emails ____

How am I feeling this morning and why?

____

____

____

____

Top 2 Priorities and Focus for today

____

____

____

My Personal Growth and Development Goals for today

____

____

____

Team Collaboration Notes Who did I support or collaborate with today?

____

____

____

Gratitude in the Workplace What went well? Who and what am I thankful for today?

____

____

____

____

____

Goals for tomorrow

____

____

____

"Your skills and talents are needed."

Day 27

Date: ____________________

Today's Meeting & Time ____________________

Follow-Up Calls /Emails ____________________

Follow-Up Calls /Emails ____________________

How am I feeling this morning and why?

Top 2 Priorities and Focus for today

My Personal Growth and Development Goals for today

Team Collaboration Notes Who did I support or collaborate with today?

Gratitude in the Workplace What went well? Who and what am I thankful for today?

Goals for tomorrow

"Mistakes are meant to be made. You don't have to be perfect to be great."

Day 28

Date: ____________________

Today's Meeting & Time ____

Follow-Up Calls /Emails ____

Follow-Up Calls /Emails ____

How am I feeling this morning and why?

____

____

____

____

Top 2 Priorities and Focus for today

____

____

____

My Personal Growth and Development Goals for today

____

____

____

Team Collaboration Notes Who did I support or collaborate with today?

____

____

____

Gratitude in the Workplace What went well? Who and what am I thankful for today?

____

____

____

____

____

Goals for tomorrow

____

____

____

"The way to get started is to begin."

Day 29

Date: ____________________

Today's Meeting & Time ____

Follow-Up Calls /Emails ____

Follow-Up Calls /Emails ____

How am I feeling this morning and why?

____

____

____

____

Top 2 Priorities and Focus for today

____

____

____

My Personal Growth and Development Goals for today

____

____

____

Team Collaboration Notes Who did I support or collaborate with today?

____

____

____

Gratitude in the Workplace What went well? Who and what am I thankful for today?

____

____

____

____

____

Goals for tomorrow

____

____

____

"It always seems impossible until it's done."

Day 30

Date: ______________________

Today's Meeting & Time ____

Follow-Up Calls /Emails ____

Follow-Up Calls /Emails ____

How am I feeling this morning and why?

____
____
____
____

Top 2 Priorities and Focus for today

____
____
____

My Personal Growth and Development Goals for today

____
____
____

Team Collaboration Notes Who did I support or collaborate with today?

____
____
____

Gratitude in the Workplace What went well? Who and what am I thankful for today?

____
____
____
____
____

Goals for tomorrow

____
____
____

"Progress, not perfection"

Day 31

Date: ______________________

Today's Meeting & Time ____

Follow-Up Calls /Emails ____

Follow-Up Calls /Emails ____

How am I feeling this morning and why?

____

____

____

____

Top 2 Priorities and Focus for today

____

____

____

My Personal Growth and Development Goals for today

____

____

____

Team Collaboration Notes Who did I support or collaborate with today?

____

____

____

Gratitude in the Workplace What went well? Who and what am I thankful for today?

____

____

____

____

____

Goals for tomorrow

____

____

____

"Growth is Daily"

Day 1

Date: ______________________

Today's Meeting & Time ____

Follow-Up Calls /Emails ____

Follow-Up Calls /Emails ____

How am I feeling this morning and why?

____

____

____

____

Top 2 Priorities and Focus for today

____

____

____

My Personal Growth and Development Goals for today

____

____

____

Team Collaboration Notes Who did I support or collaborate with today?

____

____

____

Gratitude in the Workplace What went well? Who and what am I thankful for today?

____

____

____

____

____

Goals for tomorrow

____

____

____

"Success is the sum of small efforts, repeated day in and day out."

Day 2

Date: ____________________

Today's Meeting & Time ____________________

Follow-Up Calls /Emails ____________________

Follow-Up Calls /Emails ____________________

How am I feeling this morning and why?

____

____

____

____

Top 2 Priorities and Focus for today

____

____

____

My Personal Growth and Development Goals for today

____

____

____

Team Collaboration Notes Who did I support or collaborate with today?

____

____

____

Gratitude in the Workplace What went well? Who and what am I thankful for today?

____

____

____

____

____

Goals for tomorrow

____

____

____

"The only way to do great work is to love what you do."

Day 3

Date: ______________________

Today's Meeting & Time ____

Follow-Up Calls /Emails ____

Follow-Up Calls /Emails ____

How am I feeling this morning and why?

____

____

____

____

Top 2 Priorities and Focus for today

____

____

____

My Personal Growth and Development Goals for today

____

____

____

Team Collaboration Notes Who did I support or collaborate with today?

____

____

____

Gratitude in the Workplace What went well? Who and what am I thankful for today?

____

____

____

____

____

Goals for tomorrow

____

____

____

"Believe you can and you're halfway there."

Day 4

Date: ______________________

Today's Meeting & Time ____

Follow-Up Calls /Emails ____

Follow-Up Calls /Emails ____

How am I feeling this morning and why?

____

____

____

____

Top 2 Priorities and Focus for today

____

____

____

My Personal Growth and Development Goals for today

____

____

____

Team Collaboration Notes Who did I support or collaborate with today?

____

____

____

Gratitude in the Workplace What went well? Who and what am I thankful for today?

____

____

____

____

____

Goals for tomorrow

____

____

____

"Don't watch the clock; do what it does. Keep going."

Day 5

Date: ______________________

Today's Meeting & Time ______________________

Follow-Up Calls /Emails ______________________

Follow-Up Calls /Emails ______________________

How am I feeling this morning and why?

____

Top 2 Priorities and Focus for today

____

My Personal Growth and Development Goals for today

____

Team Collaboration Notes Who did I support or collaborate with today?

____

Gratitude in the Workplace What went well? Who and what am I thankful for today?

____

Goals for tomorrow

____

"Hard work beats talent when talent doesn't work hard."

Day 6

Date: ____________________

Today's Meeting & Time ____________________

Follow-Up Calls /Emails ____________________

Follow-Up Calls /Emails ____________________

How am I feeling this morning and why?

____

____

____

____

Top 2 Priorities and Focus for today

____

____

____

My Personal Growth and Development Goals for today

____

____

____

Team Collaboration Notes Who did I support or collaborate with today?

____

____

____

Gratitude in the Workplace What went well? Who and what am I thankful for today?

____

____

____

____

____

Goals for tomorrow

____

____

____

"Your work is going to fill a large part of your life."

Day 7

Date: ______________________

Today's Meeting & Time ____

Follow-Up Calls /Emails ____

Follow-Up Calls /Emails ____

How am I feeling this morning and why?

Top 2 Priorities and Focus for today

My Personal Growth and Development Goals for today

Team Collaboration Notes Who did I support or collaborate with today?

Gratitude in the Workplace What went well? Who and what am I thankful for today?

Goals for tomorrow

"Excellence is not a skill. It is an attitude."

Day 8

Date: ______________________

Today's Meeting & Time ____

Follow-Up Calls /Emails ____

Follow-Up Calls /Emails ____

How am I feeling this morning and why?

____
____
____
____

Top 2 Priorities and Focus for today

____
____
____

My Personal Growth and Development Goals for today

____
____
____

Team Collaboration Notes Who did I support or collaborate with today?

____
____
____

Gratitude in the Workplace What went well? Who and what am I thankful for today?

____
____
____
____
____

Goals for tomorrow

____
____
____

"Quality means doing it right when no one is looking"

Day 9

Date: ______________________

Today's Meeting & Time ____

Follow-Up Calls /Emails ____

Follow-Up Calls /Emails ____

How am I feeling this morning and why?

____

____

____

____

Top 2 Priorities and Focus for today

____

____

____

My Personal Growth and Development Goals for today

____

____

____

Team Collaboration Notes Who did I support or collaborate with today?

____

____

____

Gratitude in the Workplace What went well? Who and what am I thankful for today?

____

____

____

____

____

Goals for tomorrow

____

____

____

"The best way to predict the future is to create it."

Day 10

Date: ______________________

Today's Meeting & Time ____

Follow-Up Calls /Emails ____

Follow-Up Calls /Emails ____

How am I feeling this morning and why?

____

____

____

____

Top 2 Priorities and Focus for today

____

____

____

My Personal Growth and Development Goals for today

____

____

____

Team Collaboration Notes Who did I support or collaborate with today?

____

____

____

Gratitude in the Workplace What went well? Who and what am thankful for today?

____

____

____

____

____

Goals for tomorrow

____

____

____

"Act as if what you do makes a difference. It does."

Day 11

Date: ______________________

Today's Meeting & Time ____

Follow-Up Calls /Emails ____

Follow-Up Calls /Emails ____

How am I feeling this morning and why?

____

____

____

____

Top 2 Priorities and Focus for today

____

____

____

My Personal Growth and Development Goals for today

____

____

____

Team Collaboration Notes Who did I support or collaborate with today?

____

____

____

Gratitude in the Workplace What went well? Who and what am I thankful for today?

____

____

____

____

____

Goals for tomorrow

____

____

____

"Strive not to be a success, but rather to be aof value."

Day 12

Date: ______________________

Today's Meeting & Time ____

Follow-Up Calls /Emails ____

Follow-Up Calls /Emails ____

How am I feeling this morning and why?

____

____

____

____

Top 2 Priorities and Focus for today

____

____

____

My Personal Growth and Development Goals for today

____

____

____

Team Collaboration Notes Who did I support or collaborate with today?

____

____

____

Gratitude in the Workplace What went well? Who and what am I thankful for today?

____

____

____

____

____

Goals for tomorrow

____

____

____

"Success usually comes to those who are too busy to be looking for it."

Day 13

Date: ______________________

Today's Meeting & Time ____

Follow-Up Calls /Emails ____

Follow-Up Calls /Emails ____

How am I feeling this morning and why?

____

____

____

____

Top 2 Priorities and Focus for today

____

____

____

My Personal Growth and Development Goals for today

____

____

____

Team Collaboration Notes Who did I support or collaborate with today?

____

____

____

Gratitude in the Workplace What went well? Who and what am I thankful for today?

____

____

____

____

____

Goals for tomorrow

____

____

____

"The harder you work for something, the greater you'll feel when you achieve it."

Day 14

Date: ____________________

Today's Meeting & Time ____________________

Follow-Up Calls /Emails ____________________

Follow-Up Calls /Emails ____________________

How am I feeling this morning and why?

____
____
____
____

Top 2 Priorities and Focus for today

____
____
____

My Personal Growth and Development Goals for today

____
____
____

Team Collaboration Notes Who did I support or collaborate with today?

____
____
____

Gratitude in the Workplace What went well? Who and what am I thankful for today?

____
____
____
____
____

Goals for tomorrow

____
____
____

"Success isn't just about what you accomplish, but what you inspire others to do."

Day 15

Date: ____________________

Today's Meeting & Time ____

Follow-Up Calls /Emails ____

Follow-Up Calls /Emails ____

How am I feeling this morning and why?

____

____

____

____

Top 2 Priorities and Focus for today

____

____

____

My Personal Growth and Development Goals for today

____

____

____

Team Collaboration Notes Who did I support or collaborate with today?

____

____

____

Gratitude in the Workplace What went well? Who and what am I thankful for today?

____

____

____

____

____

Goals for tomorrow

____

____

____

"Opportunities don't happen. You create them."

Day 16

Date: ____________________

Today's Meeting & Time ____________________

Follow-Up Calls /Emails ____________________

Follow-Up Calls /Emails ____________________

How am I feeling this morning and why?

____

____

____

____

Top 2 Priorities and Focus for today

____

____

____

My Personal Growth and Development Goals for today

____

____

____

Team Collaboration Notes Who did I support or collaborate with today?

____

____

____

Gratitude in the Workplace What went well? Who and what am I thankful for today?

____

____

____

____

____

Goals for tomorrow

____

____

____

"Don't limit your challenges. Challenge your limits."

Day 17

Date: ______________________

Today's Meeting & Time ______________________

Follow-Up Calls /Emails ______________________

Follow-Up Calls /Emails ______________________

How am I feeling this morning and why?

Top 2 Priorities and Focus for today

My Personal Growth and Development Goals for today

Team Collaboration Notes Who did I support or collaborate with today?

Gratitude in the Workplace What went well? Who and what am I thankful for today?

Goals for tomorrow

"Dream big."

Day 18

Date: ______________________

Today's Meeting & Time ____

Follow-Up Calls /Emails ____

Follow-Up Calls /Emails ____

How am I feeling this morning and why?

____
____
____
____

Top 2 Priorities and Focus for today

____
____
____

My Personal Growth and Development Goals for today

____
____
____

Team Collaboration Notes Who did I support or collaborate with today?

____
____
____

Gratitude in the Workplace What went well? Who and what am I thankful for today?

____
____
____
____
____

Goals for tomorrow

____
____
____

"Each day is a canvas for your masterpiece."

Day 19

Date: ____________________

Today's Meeting & Time ____________________

Follow-Up Calls /Emails ____________________

Follow-Up Calls /Emails ____________________

How am I feeling this morning and why?

Top 2 Priorities and Focus for today

My Personal Growth and Development Goals for today

Team Collaboration Notes Who did I support or collaborate with today?

Gratitude in the Workplace What went well? Who and what am I thankful for today?

Goals for tomorrow

"Great things never come from comfort zones."

Day 20

Date: ______________________

Today's Meeting & Time ____

Follow-Up Calls /Emails ____

Follow-Up Calls /Emails ____

How am I feeling this morning and why?

____

____

____

____

Top 2 Priorities and Focus for today

____

____

____

My Personal Growth and Development Goals for today

____

____

____

Team Collaboration Notes Who did I support or collaborate with today?

____

____

____

Gratitude in the Workplace What went well? Who and what am I thankful for today?

____

____

____

____

____

Goals for tomorrow

____

____

____

"Push yourself, because no one else is going to do it for you."

Day 21

Date: ____________________

Today's Meeting & Time ____

Follow-Up Calls /Emails ____

Follow-Up Calls /Emails ____

How am I feeling this morning and why?

____

____

____

____

Top 2 Priorities and Focus for today

____

____

____

My Personal Growth and Development Goals for today

____

____

____

Team Collaboration Notes Who did I support or collaborate with today?

____

____

____

Gratitude in the Workplace What went well? Who and what am I thankful for today?

____

____

____

____

____

Goals for tomorrow

____

____

____

"Your limitation - it's up to you."

Day 22

Date: ______________________

Today's Meeting & Time ____

Follow-Up Calls /Emails ____

Follow-Up Calls /Emails ____

How am I feeling this morning and why?

____

____

____

____

Top 2 Priorities and Focus for today

____

____

____

My Personal Growth and Development Goals for today

____

____

____

Team Collaboration Notes Who did I support or collaborate with today?

____

____

____

Gratitude in the Workplace What went well? Who and what am I thankful for today?

____

____

____

____

____

Goals for tomorrow

____

____

____

"Sometimes later becomes never. Act now."

Day 23

Date: ____________________

Today's Meeting & Time ____________________

Follow-Up Calls /Emails ____________________

Follow-Up Calls /Emails ____________________

How am I feeling this morning and why?

____

____

____

____

Top 2 Priorities and Focus for today

____

____

____

My Personal Growth and Development Goals for today

____

____

____

Team Collaboration Notes Who did I support or collaborate with today?

____

____

____

Gratitude in the Workplace What went well? Who and what am I thankful for today?

____

____

____

____

____

Goals for tomorrow

____

____

____

"Work in silence, and let your success be your noise."

Day 24

Date: ____________________

Today's Meeting & Time ______________________________

Follow-Up Calls /Emails ______________________________

Follow-Up Calls /Emails ______________________________

How am I feeling this morning and why?

____

____

____

____

Top 2 Priorities and Focus for today

____

____

____

My Personal Growth and Development Goals for today

____

____

____

Team Collaboration Notes Who did I support or collaborate with today?

____

____

____

Gratitude in the Workplace What went well? Who and what am I thankful for today?

____

____

____

____

____

Goals for tomorrow

____

____

____

"Don't be busy, be productive."

Day 25

Date: ____________________

Today's Meeting & Time ____________________

Follow-Up Calls /Emails ____________________

Follow-Up Calls /Emails ____________________

How am I feeling this morning and why?

____

____

____

____

Top 2 Priorities and Focus for today

____

____

____

My Personal Growth and Development Goals for today

____

____

____

Team Collaboration Notes Who did I support or collaborate with today?

____

____

____

Gratitude in the Workplace What went well? Who and what am I thankful for today?

____

____

____

____

____

Goals for tomorrow

____

____

____

"Big moves begin with small steps."

Day 26

Date: ____________________

Today's Meeting & Time ____

Follow-Up Calls /Emails ____

Follow-Up Calls /Emails ____

How am I feeling this morning and why?

____
____
____
____

Top 2 Priorities and Focus for today

____
____
____

My Personal Growth and Development Goals for today

____
____
____

Team Collaboration Notes Who did I support or collaborate with today?

____
____
____

Gratitude in the Workplace What went well? Who and what am I thankful for today?

____
____
____
____
____

Goals for tomorrow

____
____
____

"Your skills and talents are needed."

Day 27

Date: ____________________

Today's Meeting & Time ____________________

Follow-Up Calls /Emails ____________________

Follow-Up Calls /Emails ____________________

How am I feeling this morning and why?

____
____
____
____

Top 2 Priorities and Focus for today

____
____
____

My Personal Growth and Development Goals for today

____
____
____

Team Collaboration Notes Who did I support or collaborate with today?

____
____
____

Gratitude in the Workplace What went well? Who and what am I thankful for today?

____
____
____
____
____

Goals for tomorrow

____
____
____

"Mistakes are meant to be made. You don't have to be perfect to be great."

Day 28

Date: ____________________

Today's Meeting & Time ____________________

Follow-Up Calls /Emails ____________________

Follow-Up Calls /Emails ____________________

How am I feeling this morning and why?

____

____

____

____

Top 2 Priorities and Focus for today

____

____

____

My Personal Growth and Development Goals for today

____

____

____

Team Collaboration Notes Who did I support or collaborate with today?

____

____

____

Gratitude in the Workplace What went well? Who and what am I thankful for today?

____

____

____

____

____

Goals for tomorrow

____

____

____

"The way to get started is to begin."

Day 29

Date: ______________________

Today's Meeting & Time ____

Follow-Up Calls /Emails ____

Follow-Up Calls /Emails ____

How am I feeling this morning and why?

____

____

____

____

Top 2 Priorities and Focus for today

____

____

____

My Personal Growth and Development Goals for today

____

____

____

Team Collaboration Notes Who did I support or collaborate with today?

____

____

____

Gratitude in the Workplace What went well? Who and what am I thankful for today?

____

____

____

____

____

Goals for tomorrow

____

____

____

"It always seems impossible until it's done."

Day 30

Date: ____________________

Today's Meeting & Time ____________________

Follow-Up Calls /Emails ____________________

Follow-Up Calls /Emails ____________________

How am I feeling this morning and why?

____
____
____
____

Top 2 Priorities and Focus for today

____
____
____

My Personal Growth and Development Goals for today

____
____
____

Team Collaboration Notes Who did I support or collaborate with today?

____
____
____

Gratitude in the Workplace What went well? Who and what am I thankful for today?

____
____
____
____
____

Goals for tomorrow

____
____
____

"Progress, not perfection"

Day 31

Date: ______________________

Today's Meeting & Time ____

Follow-Up Calls /Emails ____

Follow-Up Calls /Emails ____

How am I feeling this morning and why?

____
____
____
____

Top 2 Priorities and Focus for today

____
____
____

My Personal Growth and Development Goals for today

____
____
____

Team Collaboration Notes Who did I support or collaborate with today?

____
____
____

Gratitude in the Workplace What went well? Who and what am I thankful for today?

____
____
____
____
____

Goals for tomorrow

____
____
____

"Growth is Daily"

Day 1

Date: ____________________

Today's Meeting & Time ____

Follow-Up Calls /Emails ____

Follow-Up Calls /Emails ____

How am I feeling this morning and why?

____

____

____

____

Top 2 Priorities and Focus for today

____

____

____

My Personal Growth and Development Goals for today

____

____

____

Team Collaboration Notes Who did I support or collaborate with today?

____

____

____

Gratitude in the Workplace What went well? Who and what am I thankful for today?

____

____

____

____

____

Goals for tomorrow

____

____

____

"Success is the sum of small efforts, repeated day in and day out."

Day 2

Date: ________________________

Today's Meeting & Time ____

Follow-Up Calls /Emails ____

Follow-Up Calls /Emails ____

How am I feeling this morning and why?

____

____

____

____

Top 2 Priorities and Focus for today

____

____

____

My Personal Growth and Development Goals for today

____

____

____

Team Collaboration Notes Who did I support or collaborate with today?

____

____

____

Gratitude in the Workplace What went well? Who and what am I thankful for today?

____

____

____

____

____

Goals for tomorrow

____

____

____

"The only way to do great work is to love what you do."

Day 3

Date: ______________________

Today's Meeting & Time ______________________

Follow-Up Calls /Emails ______________________

Follow-Up Calls /Emails ______________________

How am I feeling this morning and why?

____

____

____

____

Top 2 Priorities and Focus for today

____

____

____

My Personal Growth and Development Goals for today

____

____

____

Team Collaboration Notes Who did I support or collaborate with today?

____

____

____

Gratitude in the Workplace What went well? Who and what am I thankful for today?

____

____

____

____

____

Goals for tomorrow

____

____

____

"Believe you can and you're halfway there."

Day 4

Date: ______________________

Today's Meeting & Time ____

Follow-Up Calls /Emails ____

Follow-Up Calls /Emails ____

How am I feeling this morning and why?

____

____

____

____

Top 2 Priorities and Focus for today

____

____

____

My Personal Growth and Development Goals for today

____

____

____

Team Collaboration Notes Who did I support or collaborate with today?

____

____

____

Gratitude in the Workplace What went well? Who and what am I thankful for today?

____

____

____

____

____

Goals for tomorrow

____

____

____

"Don't watch the clock; do what it does. Keep going."

Day 5

Date: ____________________

Today's Meeting & Time ____________________

Follow-Up Calls /Emails ____________________

Follow-Up Calls /Emails ____________________

How am I feeling this morning and why?

____
____
____
____

Top 2 Priorities and Focus for today

____
____
____

My Personal Growth and Development Goals for today

____
____
____

Team Collaboration Notes Who did I support or collaborate with today?

____
____
____

Gratitude in the Workplace What went well? Who and what am I thankful for today?

____
____
____
____
____

Goals for tomorrow

____
____
____

"Hard work beats talent when talent doesn't work hard."

Day 6

Date: ______________________

Today's Meeting & Time ____

Follow-Up Calls /Emails ____

Follow-Up Calls /Emails ____

How am I feeling this morning and why?

Top 2 Priorities and Focus for today

My Personal Growth and Development Goals for today

Team Collaboration Notes Who did I support or collaborate with today?

Gratitude in the Workplace What went well? Who and what am I thankful for today?

Goals for tomorrow

"Your work is going to fill a large part of your life."

Day 7

Date: ______________________

Today's Meeting & Time ____

Follow-Up Calls /Emails ____

Follow-Up Calls /Emails ____

How am I feeling this morning and why?

____
____
____
____

Top 2 Priorities and Focus for today

____
____
____

My Personal Growth and Development Goals for today

____
____
____

Team Collaboration Notes Who did I support or collaborate with today?

____
____
____

Gratitude in the Workplace What went well? Who and what am I thankful for today?

____
____
____
____
____

Goals for tomorrow

____
____
____

"Excellence is not a skill. It is an attitude."

Day 8

Date: ______________________

Today's Meeting & Time ____

Follow-Up Calls /Emails ____

Follow-Up Calls /Emails ____

How am I feeling this morning and why?

____

____

____

____

Top 2 Priorities and Focus for today

____

____

____

My Personal Growth and Development Goals for today

____

____

____

Team Collaboration Notes Who did I support or collaborate with today?

____

____

____

Gratitude in the Workplace What went well? Who and what am I thankful for today?

____

____

____

____

____

Goals for tomorrow

____

____

____

"Quality means doing it right when no one is looking."

Day 9

Date: ______________________

Today's Meeting & Time ____

Follow-Up Calls /Emails ____

Follow-Up Calls /Emails ____

How am I feeling this morning and why?

____

____

____

____

Top 2 Priorities and Focus for today

____

____

____

My Personal Growth and Development Goals for today

____

____

____

Team Collaboration Notes Who did I support or collaborate with today?

____

____

____

Gratitude in the Workplace What went well? Who and what am I thankful for today?

____

____

____

____

____

Goals for tomorrow

____

____

____

"The best way to predict the future is to create it."

Day 10

Date: ______________________

Today's Meeting & Time ____

Follow-Up Calls /Emails ____

Follow-Up Calls /Emails ____

How am I feeling this morning and why?

____

____

____

____

Top 2 Priorities and Focus for today

____

____

____

My Personal Growth and Development Goals for today

____

____

____

Team Collaboration Notes Who did I support or collaborate with today?

____

____

____

Gratitude in the Workplace What went well? Who and what am I thankful for today?

____

____

____

____

____

Goals for tomorrow

____

____

____

"Act as if what you do makes a difference. It does."

Day 11

Date: ____________________

Today's Meeting & Time ____

Follow-Up Calls /Emails ____

Follow-Up Calls /Emails ____

How am I feeling this morning and why?

____

____

____

____

Top 2 Priorities and Focus for today

____

____

____

My Personal Growth and Development Goals for today

____

____

____

Team Collaboration Notes Who did I support or collaborate with today?

____

____

____

Gratitude in the Workplace What went well? Who and what am I thankful for today?

____

____

____

____

____

Goals for tomorrow

____

____

____

"Strive not to be a success, but rather to be aof value."

Day 12

Date: ____________________

Today's Meeting & Time ____

Follow-Up Calls /Emails ____

Follow-Up Calls /Emails ____

How am I feeling this morning and why?

____
____
____
____

Top 2 Priorities and Focus for today

____
____
____

My Personal Growth and Development Goals for today

____
____
____

Team Collaboration Notes Who did I support or collaborate with today?

____
____
____

Gratitude in the Workplace What went well? Who and what am I thankful for today?

____
____
____
____
____

Goals for tomorrow

____
____
____

"Success usually comes to those who are too busy to be looking for it."

Day 13

Date: ____________________

Today's Meeting & Time ____________________

Follow-Up Calls /Emails ____________________

Follow-Up Calls /Emails ____________________

How am I feeling this morning and why?

____

____

____

____

Top 2 Priorities and Focus for today

____

____

____

My Personal Growth and Development Goals for today

____

____

____

Team Collaboration Notes Who did I support or collaborate with today?

____

____

____

Gratitude in the Workplace What went well? Who and what am I thankful for today?

____

____

____

____

____

Goals for tomorrow

____

____

____

"The harder you work for something, the greater you'll feel when you achieve it."

Day 14

Date: ______________________

Today's Meeting & Time ____

Follow-Up Calls /Emails ____

Follow-Up Calls /Emails ____

How am I feeling this morning and why?

____

____

____

____

Top 2 Priorities and Focus for today

____

____

____

My Personal Growth and Development Goals for today

____

____

____

Team Collaboration Notes Who did I support or collaborate with today?

____

____

____

Gratitude in the Workplace What went well? Who and what am I thankful for today?

____

____

____

____

____

Goals for tomorrow

____

____

____

"Success isn't just about what you accomplish, but what you inspire others to do."

Day 15

Date: ______________________

Today's Meeting & Time ____

Follow-Up Calls /Emails ____

Follow-Up Calls /Emails ____

How am I feeling this morning and why?

____

____

____

____

Top 2 Priorities and Focus for today

____

____

____

My Personal Growth and Development Goals for today

____

____

____

Team Collaboration Notes Who did I support or collaborate with today?

____

____

____

Gratitude in the Workplace What went well? Who and what am I thankful for today?

____

____

____

____

____

Goals for tomorrow

____

____

____

"Opportunities don't happen. You create them."

Day 16

Date: ______________________

Today's Meeting & Time ____

Follow-Up Calls /Emails ____

Follow-Up Calls /Emails ____

How am I feeling this morning and why?

____

____

____

____

Top 2 Priorities and Focus for today

____

____

____

My Personal Growth and Development Goals for today

____

____

____

Team Collaboration Notes Who did I support or collaborate with today?

____

____

____

Gratitude in the Workplace What went well? Who and what am I thankful for today?

____

____

____

____

____

Goals for tomorrow

____

____

____

"Don't limit your challenges. Challenge your limits."

Day 17

Date: ____________________

Today's Meeting & Time ____________________

Follow-Up Calls /Emails ____________________

Follow-Up Calls /Emails ____________________

How am I feeling this morning and why?

Top 2 Priorities and Focus for today

My Personal Growth and Development Goals for today

Team Collaboration Notes Who did I support or collaborate with today?

Gratitude in the Workplace What went well? Who and what am I thankful for today?

Goals for tomorrow

"Dream big."

Day 18

Date: ____________________

Today's Meeting & Time ____________________

Follow-Up Calls /Emails ____________________

Follow-Up Calls /Emails ____________________

How am I feeling this morning and why?

____

____

____

____

Top 2 Priorities and Focus for today

____

____

____

My Personal Growth and Development Goals for today

____

____

____

Team Collaboration Notes Who did I support or collaborate with today?

____

____

____

Gratitude in the Workplace What went well? Who and what am I thankful for today?

____

____

____

____

____

Goals for tomorrow

____

____

____

"Each day is a canvas for your masterpiece."

Day 19

Date: ____________________

Today's Meeting & Time ____

Follow-Up Calls /Emails ____

Follow-Up Calls /Emails ____

How am I feeling this morning and why?

____

____

____

____

Top 2 Priorities and Focus for today

____

____

____

My Personal Growth and Development Goals for today

____

____

____

Team Collaboration Notes Who did I support or collaborate with today?

____

____

____

Gratitude in the Workplace What went well? Who and what am I thankful for today?

____

____

____

____

____

Goals for tomorrow

____

____

____

"Great things never come from comfort zones."

Day 20

Date: ______________________

Today's Meeting & Time ____

Follow-Up Calls /Emails ____

Follow-Up Calls /Emails ____

How am I feeling this morning and why?

____

____

____

____

Top 2 Priorities and Focus for today

____

____

____

My Personal Growth and Development Goals for today

____

____

____

Team Collaboration Notes Who did I support or collaborate with today?

____

____

____

Gratitude in the Workplace What went well? Who and what am I thankful for today?

____

____

____

____

____

Goals for tomorrow

____

____

____

"Push yourself, because no one else is going to do it for you."

Day 21

Date: ____________________

Today's Meeting & Time ____________________

Follow-Up Calls /Emails ____________________

Follow-Up Calls /Emails ____________________

How am I feeling this morning and why?

Top 2 Priorities and Focus for today

My Personal Growth and Development Goals for today

Team Collaboration Notes Who did I support or collaborate with today?

Gratitude in the Workplace What went well? Who and what am I thankful for today?

Goals for tomorrow

"Your limitation - it's up to you."

Day 22

Date: ______________________

Today's Meeting & Time ____

Follow-Up Calls /Emails ____

Follow-Up Calls /Emails ____

How am I feeling this morning and why?

____

____

____

____

Top 2 Priorities and Focus for today

____

____

____

My Personal Growth and Development Goals for today

____

____

____

Team Collaboration Notes Who did I support or collaborate with today?

____

____

____

Gratitude in the Workplace What went well? Who and what am I thankful for today?

____

____

____

____

____

Goals for tomorrow

____

____

____

"Sometimes later becomes never. Act now."

Day 23

Date: ______________________

Today's Meeting & Time ____

Follow-Up Calls /Emails ____

Follow-Up Calls /Emails ____

How am I feeling this morning and why?

____

____

____

____

Top 2 Priorities and Focus for today

____

____

____

My Personal Growth and Development Goals for today

____

____

____

Team Collaboration Notes Who did I support or collaborate with today?

____

____

____

Gratitude in the Workplace What went well? Who and what am I thankful for today?

____

____

____

____

____

Goals for tomorrow

____

____

____

"Work in silence, and let your success be your noise."

Day 24

Date: ______________________

Today's Meeting & Time ____

Follow-Up Calls /Emails ____

Follow-Up Calls /Emails ____

How am I feeling this morning and why?

____

____

____

____

Top 2 Priorities and Focus for today

____

____

____

My Personal Growth and Development Goals for today

____

____

____

Team Collaboration Notes Who did I support or collaborate with today?

____

____

____

Gratitude in the Workplace What went well? Who and what am I thankful for today?

____

____

____

____

____

Goals for tomorrow

____

____

____

"Don't be busy, be productive."

Day 25

Date: ______________________

Today's Meeting & Time ____

Follow-Up Calls /Emails ____

Follow-Up Calls /Emails ____

How am I feeling this morning and why?

____
____
____
____

Top 2 Priorities and Focus for today

____
____
____

My Personal Growth and Development Goals for today

____
____
____

Team Collaboration Notes Who did I support or collaborate with today?

____
____
____

Gratitude in the Workplace What went well? Who and what am I thankful for today?

____
____
____
____
____

Goals for tomorrow

____
____
____

"Big moves begin with small steps."

Day 26

Date: ____________________

Today's Meeting & Time ____

Follow-Up Calls /Emails ____

Follow-Up Calls /Emails ____

How am I feeling this morning and why?

____

____

____

____

Top 2 Priorities and Focus for today

____

____

____

My Personal Growth and Development Goals for today

____

____

____

Team Collaboration Notes Who did I support or collaborate with today?

____

____

____

Gratitude in the Workplace What went well? Who and what am I thankful for today?

____

____

____

____

____

Goals for tomorrow

____

____

____

"Your skills and talents are needed."

Day 27

Date: ____________________

Today's Meeting & Time ____________________

Follow-Up Calls /Emails ____________________

Follow-Up Calls /Emails ____________________

How am I feeling this morning and why?

____

____

____

____

Top 2 Priorities and Focus for today

____

____

____

My Personal Growth and Development Goals for today

____

____

____

Team Collaboration Notes Who did I support or collaborate with today?

____

____

____

Gratitude in the Workplace What went well? Who and what am I thankful for today?

____

____

____

____

____

Goals for tomorrow

____

____

____

"Mistakes are meant to be made. You don't have to be perfect to be great."

Day 28

Date: ______________________

Today's Meeting & Time ____

Follow-Up Calls /Emails ____

Follow-Up Calls /Emails ____

How am I feeling this morning and why?

____

____

____

____

Top 2 Priorities and Focus for today

____

____

____

My Personal Growth and Development Goals for today

____

____

____

Team Collaboration Notes Who did I support or collaborate with today?

____

____

____

Gratitude in the Workplace What went well? Who and what am I thankful for today?

____

____

____

____

____

Goals for tomorrow

____

____

____

"The way to get started is to begin."

Day 29

Date: ____________________

Today's Meeting & Time ____________________

Follow-Up Calls /Emails ____________________

Follow-Up Calls /Emails ____________________

How am I feeling this morning and why?

____

____

____

____

Top 2 Priorities and Focus for today

____

____

____

My Personal Growth and Development Goals for today

____

____

____

Team Collaboration Notes Who did I support or collaborate with today?

____

____

____

Gratitude in the Workplace What went well? Who and what am I thankful for today?

____

____

____

____

____

Goals for tomorrow

____

____

____

"It always seems impossible until it's done."

Day 30

Date: ____________________

Today's Meeting & Time ____________________

Follow-Up Calls /Emails ____________________

Follow-Up Calls /Emails ____________________

How am I feeling this morning and why?

____

____

____

____

Top 2 Priorities and Focus for today

____

____

____

My Personal Growth and Development Goals for today

____

____

____

Team Collaboration Notes Who did I support or collaborate with today?

____

____

____

Gratitude in the Workplace What went well? Who and what am I thankful for today?

____

____

____

____

____

Goals for tomorrow

____

____

____

"Progress, not perfection"

Day 31

Date: ____________________

Today's Meeting & Time ____________________

Follow-Up Calls /Emails ____________________

Follow-Up Calls /Emails ____________________

How am I feeling this morning and why?

____

____

____

____

Top 2 Priorities and Focus for today

____

____

____

My Personal Growth and Development Goals for today

____

____

____

Team Collaboration Notes Who did I support or collaborate with today?

____

____

____

Gratitude in the Workplace What went well? Who and what am I thankful for today?

____

____

____

____

____

Goals for tomorrow

____

____

____

"Growth is Daily"

WEEK #1 REFLECTION

Take a moment to pause, reflect, and realign for the week aheac.

1. What milestones or goals did I reach this week? Did I celebrate?

____

____

____

2. In what ways did I grow—personally or professionally?

____

____

____

3. What went well, and why?

____

____

____

4. How did I contribute to the company and who did I support or uplift this week?

____

____

____

5. What could I improve moving forward?

____

____

____

6. What am I hoping for as I head into next week?

____

____

____

WEEK #2 REFLECTION

Take a moment to pause, reflect, and realign for the week ahead.

1. What milestones or goals did I reach this week? Did I celebrate?

____

____

____

2. In what ways did I grow—personally or professionally?

____

____

____

3. What went well, and why?

____

____

____

4. How did I contribute to the company and who did I support or uplift this week?

____

____

____

5. What could I improve moving forward?

____

____

____

6. What am I hoping for as I head into next week?

____

____

____

WEEK #3 REFLECTION

Take a moment to pause, reflect, and realign for the week ahead.

1. What milestones or goals did I reach this week? Did I celebrate?

____

____

____

2. In what ways did I grow—personally or professionally?

____

____

____

3. What went well, and why?

____

____

____

4. How did I contribute to the company and who did I support or uplift this week?

____

____

____

5. What could I improve moving forward?

____

____

____

6. What am I hoping for as I head into next week?

____

____

____

WEEK #4 REFLECTION

Take a moment to pause, reflect, and realign for the week ahead.

1. What milestones or goals did I reach this week? Did I celebrate?

2. In what ways did I grow—personally or professionally?

3. What went well, and why?

4. How did I contribute to the company and who did I support or uplift this week?

5. What could I improve moving forward?

6. What am I hoping for as I head into next week?

WEEK #5 REFLECTION

Take a moment to pause, reflect, and realign for the week ahead.

1. What milestones or goals did I reach this week? Did I celebrate?

____

____

____

2. In what ways did I grow—personally or professionally?

____

____

____

3. What went well, and why?

____

____

____

4. How did I contribute to the company and who did I support or uplift this week?

____

____

____

5. What could I improve moving forward?

____

____

____

6. What am I hoping for as I head into next week?

____

____

____

WEEK #6 REFLECTION

Take a moment to pause, reflect, and realign for the week ahead.

1. What milestones or goals did I reach this week? Did I celebrate?

2. In what ways did I grow—personally or professionally?

3. What went well, and why?

4. How did I contribute to the company and who did I support or uplift this week?

5. What could I improve moving forward?

6. What am I hoping for as I head into next week?

WEEK #7 REFLECTION

Take a moment to pause, reflect, and realign for the week ahead.

1. What milestones or goals did I reach this week? Did I celebrate?

2. In what ways did I grow—personally or professionally?

3. What went well, and why?

4. How did I contribute to the company and who did I support or uplift this week?

5. What could I improve moving forward?

6. What am I hoping for as I head into next week?

WEEK #8 REFLECTION

Take a moment to pause, reflect, and realign for the week ahead.

1. What milestones or goals did I reach this week? Did I celebrate?

____

____

____

2. In what ways did I grow—personally or professionally?

____

____

____

3. What went well, and why?

____

____

____

4. How did I contribute to the company and who did I support or uplift this week?

____

____

____

5. What could I improve moving forward?

____

____

____

6. What am I hoping for as I head into next week?

____

____

____

WEEK #9 REFLECTION

Take a moment to pause, reflect, and realign for the week ahead.

1. What milestones or goals did I reach this week? Did I celebrate?

____

____

____

2. In what ways did I grow—personally or professionally?

____

____

____

3. What went well, and why?

____

____

____

4. How did I contribute to the company and who did I support or uplift this week?

____

____

____

5. What could I improve moving forward?

____

____

____

6. What am I hoping for as I head into next week?

____

____

____

WEEK #10 REFLECTION

Take a moment to pause, reflect, and realign for the week ahead.

1. What milestones or goals did I reach this week? Did I celebrate?

____

____

____

2. In what ways did I grow—personally or professionally?

____

____

____

3. What went well, and why?

____

____

____

4. How did I contribute to the company and who did I support or uplift this week?

____

____

____

5. What could I improve moving forward?

____

____

____

6. What am I hoping for as I head into next week?

____

____

____

WEEK #11 REFLECTION

Take a moment to pause, reflect, and realign for the week ahead.

1. What milestones or goals did I reach this week? Did I celebrate?

2. In what ways did I grow—personally or professionally?

3. What went well, and why?

4. How did I contribute to the company and who did I support or uplift this week?

5. What could I improve moving forward?

6. What am I hoping for as I head into next week?

WEEK #12 REFLECTION

Take a moment to pause, reflect, and realign for the week ahead.

1. What milestones or goals did I reach this week? Did I celebrate?

2. In what ways did I grow—personally or professionally?

3. What went well, and why?

4. How did I contribute to the company and who did I support or uplift this week?

5. What could I improve moving forward?

6. What am I hoping for as I head into next week?

WEEK #13 REFLECTION

Take a moment to pause, reflect, and realign for the week ahead.

1. What milestones or goals did I reach this week? Did I celebrate?

____

____

____

2. In what ways did I grow—personally or professionally?

____

____

____

3. What went well, and why?

____

____

____

4. How did I contribute to the company and who did I support or uplift this week?

____

____

____

5. What could I improve moving forward?

____

____

____

6. What am I hoping for as I head into next week?

____

____

____

WEEK #14 REFLECTION

Take a moment to pause, reflect, and realign for the week ahead.

1. What milestones or goals did I reach this week? Did I celebrate?

2. In what ways did I grow—personally or professionally?

3. What went well, and why?

4. How did I contribute to the company and who did I support or uplift this week?

5. What could I improve moving forward?

6. What am I hoping for as I head into next week?

WEEK #15 REFLECTION

Take a moment to pause, reflect, and realign for the week ahead.

1. What milestones or goals did I reach this week? Did I celebrate?

2. In what ways did I grow—personally or professionally?

3. What went well, and why?

4. How did I contribute to the company and who did I support or uplift this week?

5. What could I improve moving forward?

6. What am I hoping for as I head into next week?

Made in the USA
Monee, IL
04 November 2026

67387005R00066